KU-547-894

This book belongs to:

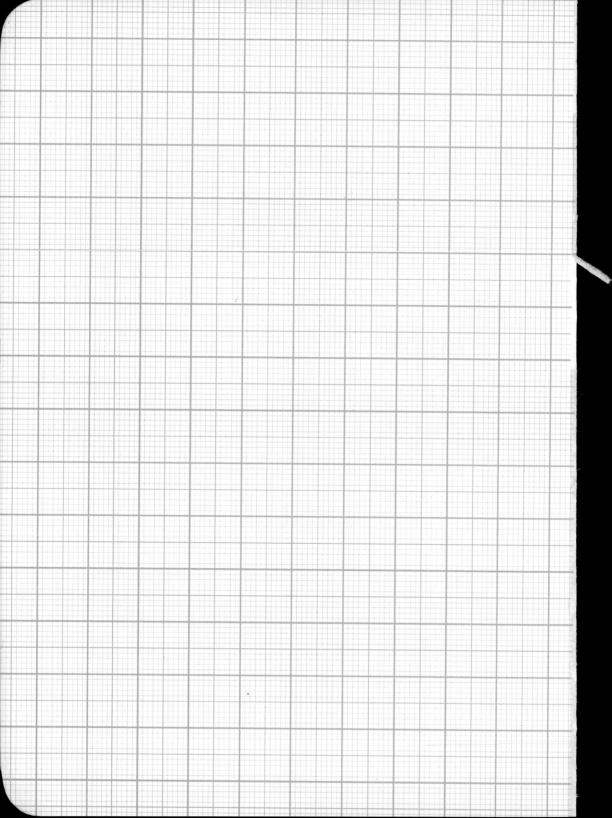

My Perfectly Imperfect Life

Also by **IRENE SMIT** and
ASTRID VAN DER HULST

• ✦ • • ✦ • •

My Perfectly IMPERFECT Life

127 Exercises in Self-Acceptance

IRENE SMIT & ASTRID VAN DER HULST

Illustrations by Karen Weening

Workman Publishing » New York

Copyright © 2019 by Sanoma Media Netherlands B.V./Flow

Illustrations copyright © 2019 by Karen Weening

All rights reserved. No portion of this book may be reproduced—mechanically, electronically, or by any other means, including photocopying—without written permission of the publisher.
Published simultaneously in Canada by Thomas Allen & Son Limited.

Library of Congress Cataloging-in-Publication Data is available.

ISBN: 978-1-5235-0636-1

Design by Rae Ann Spitzenberger
Text compiled by Caroline Buijs and Julia Gorodecky

Additional Credits: Shutterstock.com: Kjpargeter (watercolor background) pp. i, 1, 4, 7–8, 12, 14, 16, 21, 27, 29, 32, 37, 38, 51, 54, 60, 63, 71, 75, 78, 81, 97, 101, 107, 112, 115, 125, 129, 134–135, 145, 147, 151, 156, 166–168; Lina Kundzeleviciene (watercolor background) cover, endpapers, and pp. iii, 6, 11, 17–18, 33–34, 50, 57, 62, 66, 72, 79, 84–85, 90–91, 113, 116, 120–121, 128, 133, 136, 148, 152, 160, 164, 169; The Pixel (graph paper) endpapers and pp. ii, 6, 17, 23, 28, 45, 81, 84–85, 88, 107, 119, 133, 138, 150, 156, 163; Irina Zharkova (watercolor shapes) pp. 54, 66, 79, 113, 119, 128, 151.

Workman books are available at special discounts when purchased in bulk for premiums and sales promotions as well as for fund-raising or educational use. Special editions or book excerpts can also be created to specification. For details, contact the Special Sales Director at the address below, or send an email to specialmarkets@workman.com.

Workman Publishing Co., Inc.
225 Varick Street
New York, NY 10014-4381
workman.com

flowmagazine.com

FLOW is a registered trademark of Sanoma Media Netherlands B.V.

WORKMAN is a registered trademark of Workman Publishing Co., Inc.

Printed in China
First printing August 2019

Contents

Without imperfection, neither you nor I would exist.

—Stephen Hawking
THEORETICAL PHYSICIST

Introduction

Adulthood always sounded so nice as a child, but once it came, it was a bit different than we imagined. Instead of more freedom, we created new rules for ourselves. Things like: Don't ever be late. Always remember someone's birthday. Find a good job. Always have a tidy home. Eat healthy food every day. Read lots of books. Go to the theater often. Call your parents every weekend. Volunteer. Be patient. And never cancel an appointment.

Instead of being happy, we were tired. Attaining that Perfect Life didn't seem possible, but still we chased it, becoming stressed and annoyed in the constant pursuit. It was only through the mistakes, chaos, and experiences that didn't go as planned that we started to realize things became fun again when we let it go a little, when we did not have to be perfect anymore. Liking ourselves just the way we are, accepting events and situations as they come: *These* are the best life lessons (and often the most joyful).

This workbook shows you how to embrace your own Perfectly Imperfect Life. Because not everything works out. And that's not such a bad thing.

xo,

Astrid
& Irene

CHAPTER 1

My Perfectly Imperfect

WORK

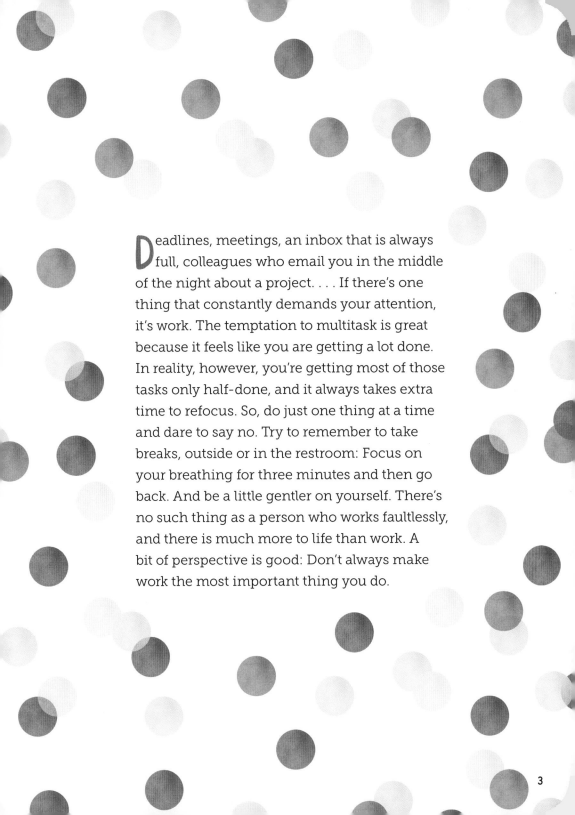

Deadlines, meetings, an inbox that is always full, colleagues who email you in the middle of the night about a project. . . . If there's one thing that constantly demands your attention, it's work. The temptation to multitask is great because it feels like you are getting a lot done. In reality, however, you're getting most of those tasks only half-done, and it always takes extra time to refocus. So, do just one thing at a time and dare to say no. Try to remember to take breaks, outside or in the restroom: Focus on your breathing for three minutes and then go back. And be a little gentler on yourself. There's no such thing as a person who works faultlessly, and there is much more to life than work. A bit of perspective is good: Don't always make work the most important thing you do.

MOVE YOUR BODY

Staying fit and slowing down go well together. Research shows that strolling around the whole day is healthier than sitting for a whole day at work or going to the gym twice a week. And though sauntering about all day may sound unrealistic, there are little ways you can fit in some exercise: Take regular walks to the watercooler or coffee machine, or stop by a colleague's desk instead of sending an email.

» Draw the routes you walked today.

BE IN THE MOMENT

Stay in the here and now. It sounds beautiful. But how does one actually do it? Here's a simple exercise to try: Whenever you encounter water in your daily activities—when you're washing your hands, watering plants, taking a shower, brushing your teeth, washing vegetables—focus not on what you're doing next, but on the moment. Is the water warm, cold, heavy, or light? What sound does it make as it drips, rushes, or splashes? It's a simple but concrete action that allows for a bit of meditation and reflection during a busy day.

>> Draw or write about your fondest memory of water. (It could be a warm bath, a lake where you enjoyed a wonderful swim, the sea where the sun shone beautifully on the waves, and so on.)

Last day of Uganda and we were playing around in lake Victoria.

When I was in Uganda and my brother took a rope swing into the sea.

According to a study by Cornell University, people with a great deal of knowledge often doubt themselves and underestimate their abilities. Ironically, less-knowledgeable people tend to overestimate their abilities. They doubt themselves less quickly, are determined, and claim they know the answer to everything. It also takes them longer to see their own errors.

>> For one week, write down all the things you doubted you could handle. When you look back at each one, do you find that your doubts were justified?

DAY 1	
DAY 2	
DAY 3	
DAY 4	
DAY 5	
DAY 6	
DAY 7	

LETTING GO OF YOUR THOUGHTS

After a busy day, our brains tend to overflow, making it hard for us to relax. It is actually at times like these, when things are far from quiet in our heads, that meditation can be very effective, even if you don't realize it until afterward. Try these techniques the next time you're feeling stressed:

- Focus your attention on something else for a moment, preferably something repetitive, such as your breathing.

- Choose a mantra, such as *I'll do it later* or *So what else is new?*

- Picture your thoughts in a specific situation. Imagine, for example, that you are throwing your thoughts over a wall. Or try seeing your thoughts as boats sailing on water, with you deciding whether to get on board or stay on the shore.

- Give each thought a label, such as "memory," "fantasy," or "worry." This helps you create distance. You are not pushing the thought away—you are simply letting it pass by.

Now is the future that you promised yourself last year, last month, last week.

—Mark Williams
AUTHOR AND PSYCHOLOGY PROFESSOR

SNAIL (E)MAIL

What are your habits when you check email? Do you tend to act on your first impulse? Take a moment before answering an email to stop and think, and decide how you want to respond. Formulate your response carefully, then read it through one more time before you hit Send.

>> Try this for a week and write down how it works for you.

>> What does it feel like to do something without rushing? Write or draw a list of what you want to do at a more leisurely pace this week (for example, walk to work instead of riding your bike, and stop and chat with someone on the way).

TAKE A BREAK

It's hard to tear yourself away from what you're working on, especially when you're engrossed in the task at hand. But it's important to take frequent breaks—they help you let go of any stress and tension that come with the task. Moreover, you might *think* you're achieving more by working nonstop, but in reality your productivity is decreasing. So take the time for that lunch outside the office, that short conversation with a friend, or that afternoon walk for a bit of fresh air.

» Draw today's lunch and your view while eating it.

THE ART OF OBSERVATION

Meditation is actually nothing more than transforming your busy, overactive mind and body into a relaxed state. Although there are a variety of ways to do this, the basic elements are focus and attention. The minute you notice you are getting distracted, calmly return your focus to the moment. If you have to, do that over and over again, dozens of times. Thoughts (about a meeting you had or the grocery shopping you have to do later), sounds (noisy traffic), and feelings (restlessness, impatience) might continue to crop up and don't have to be "banished," but the difference is that you don't have to continually get sucked into their vortex. Instead, you distance yourself from those thoughts and feelings and just observe them.

» Free up two minutes before you go into a meeting. Pay attention to how you are sitting and breathing, or be as aware as you can while walking to the meeting location. During the meeting, check in a couple of times to observe how you are sitting in your chair or how your body feels. Did this change the meeting in any way, either your thoughts about it or the outcome?

From the outside, it may seem as if I'm always working. But that's not how I look at my life. There's no "I'm here at work" and then "I'm off work." It's more like "This is what I do, and I love it all."

—Ava DuVernay

FILM DIRECTOR AND PRODUCER

TIME TO REFOCUS

Plan time in your day when you can be alone without any distractions—away from work, from family and friends, from life. Go for a walk by yourself (and leave your phone at home or in the office). Sit on a bench somewhere and let time slip right through your fingers. Let your mind be quiet for a bit. "Checking out" regularly is important. It expands our sense of time, which makes us feel less hurried and stressed.

>> Draw your favorite thing to do when you're alone.

LEND AN EAR

Are you focusing on what you want to say while your coworker is speaking? Is your mind wandering? Are you thinking about something you have to do? Make a mental note of this, and then redirect your thoughts to the other person.

>> How can you remind yourself to refocus when your attention drifts? Write down a few ideas here.

We have two ears and one mouth so that we can listen twice as much as we speak.

—Epictetus
GREEK PHILOSOPHER

CONSIDER YOUR ENERGY LEVEL

Lists are useful tools, but they shouldn't turn into an obsession. Let your list work for you and not the other way around. For example, don't start the day by doing the first item on your list without question. Be aware of your energy level. If you are at your sharpest early in the morning, don't start by answering all your email. Do something that needs plenty of focus.

>> Draw a diagram of your day, and try to identify when your energy level is lowest and when it is highest.

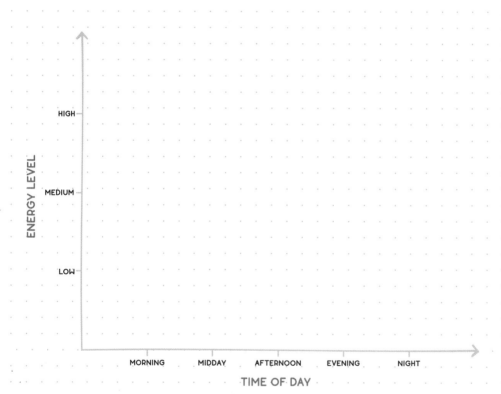

LET IT RING

Don't answer the phone the second it rings; let it ring two or three times. Move the focus to yourself, and answer the call with an open mind. If you are feeling rushed or irritated because someone is interrupting what you're doing, you can always choose not to answer and return the call later. Keep a call log and record your reaction to each one.

CALL	REACTION

QUIET YOUR MIND

It's pretty remarkable that your mind, when it's too full, can be calmed with creative tasks. Drawing, cutting paper, writing, watching a good movie, or visiting a museum—it doesn't really matter what you do. And it works the other way around, too: When you create stillness in your head, you're making space for new solutions and ideas.

>> Write down some creative tasks you would like to do more often.

gardening

AVOID MULTITASKING

If you try to do two things at the same time, your attention will be divided and you will be more likely to make mistakes. Always try to do one thing during a certain period of time, and take a short break before starting the next task. Turn off your phone and email notifications as often as you can.

>> Draw all the things that you are used to doing at the same time. Then draw them separately.

CHAPTER 2

My Perfectly Imperfect

HOME

A home is an intimate place—a sanctuary after a hard day at work, a celebratory space for birthdays and small victories, a visual reflection of your tastes and values, and much more. Because we spend so much time at home, we often want it to be perfect. But who calls the shots on the definition of "perfect"? Isn't a corridor full of thrown-off shoes much nicer than an uber-tidy entryway? Don't those worn stairs say, "The feet of happy people run up and down us dozens of times a day"? And how boring would it be to live in a house where nothing was ever moved, nothing ever fell, and nothing ever broke? These are often the things that make the best memories.

If you pay attention to your household chores while you're doing them, you can gain a great sense of satisfaction. For example, if you have to make cookies for a school event, make them with your children. Clean the windows until they shine and there are no more smears to be seen, and then notice the sun shining through them. Household chores are great opportunities to get into the here and now, and you can practice mindfulness in the comfort of your own space, without stress or distractions. Naturally, you want results—a clean house or tasty cookies—but doing housework in a mindful way is mainly about the process: giving each task your full attention and dedication without thinking about what it delivers.

» Try baking a treat just because you find it fun to play with flour and butter (not because you need to bake perfect-looking cookies). How does this experience make you feel?

me time

>> Put some tea in an old-fashioned teapot and place the teapot under a tea cozy. Draw your teapot here.

>> Buy bread from a local baker instead of the supermarket. Can you taste the difference? Is there a way to fit that into your weekly routine? Fix your bread however you like, and draw your plate with the bread and its toppings above.

S chedule yourself a day of imperfection. Then sit back and be surprised by how much lighter life feels that day. It doesn't matter if you don't do the dishes, you leave the laundry unfolded, and your children have toaster waffles for breakfast. Because today's the day it doesn't have to be perfect! The best part: Nobody else will even notice.

8 AM	
9 AM	
10 AM	
11 AM	
12 PM	
1 PM	
2 PM	
3 PM	
4 PM	
5 PM	
6 PM	

CHECK SOMETHING OFF EVERY DAY

A good tip: Split huge, daunting tasks into separate steps. For example, "paint the house" could be broken down into "sand the window frames," "select paint color," "prime the frames," and so on. That way, you can check something off every day, which feels good! And don't worry if there are things left over at the end of the week: They're the starting point for your next list.

>> Choose two big tasks from your current to-do list and break them into smaller steps here.

TASK 1		TASK 2	
☐		☐	
☐		☐	
☐		☐	
☐		☐	
☐		☐	
☐		☐	
☐		☐	
☐		☐	

JUST PICK UP THE MOP

The thing about housework is that it is never finished, and it is never perfect. In mindfulness, letting go means that you do not fixate on a certain outcome or idea about how something should be. If you have just mopped the floor and your dog or cat comes running in from the garden with muddy paws, you might become vexed about it. But you can also learn to accept that you have no control over these kinds of things—simply pick up the mop again and let your thoughts just be.

>> Try to practice this sometime during the week, and write about your experience here.

MEDITATION IN MOTION

If trying to meditate while sitting quietly on a pillow is asking too much of you, you can also try to meditate "on the go." Make a point of doing one thing every day that you focus all your attention on, such as walking up the stairs, brushing your teeth, showering, or opening a door. This gives you a few small meditation moments throughout your day. You could also prepare a slow-cooked meal, go for a walk or a swim, or do some gardening.

>> What are some activities throughout your day that could be meditative?

>> Prepare a Sunday stew with fresh herbs and vegetables from the market. Copy the recipe here and add a few lines about whether it was good, with whom you ate the meal, and what you talked about while eating.

RECIPE

Reflections

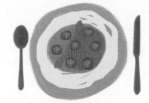

The nicest and sweetest days are not those on which anything very splendid or wonderful or exciting happens but just those that bring simple little pleasures, following one another softly, like pearls slipping off a string.

—L. M. Montgomery

AUTHOR

>> Use leftover pieces of fabric to make little bags, and fill them with dried lavender. Place the lavender bags in between items of clothing in your dresser. Tape or glue a strip of the fabric and a dried lavender flower here.

>> What other fun DIY projects could you make with found materials?

The invention of the dishwasher has made our lives easier in many ways. But it has also taken away those cozy moments when you had a pleasant chat with a family member while doing the dishes, as well as that sense of satisfaction when everything was done and the clean dishes were stacked in the cupboards.

>> Try doing the dishes by hand this week with a housemate and have a conversation while doing so. Write down what you talked about here.

_____

_____

_____

_____

_____

_____

_____

_____

_____

_____

_____

_____

_____

_____

_____

_____

BEWARE THE COMPARE

Try not to compare yourself to others for a week. Each time you become aware that you are doing it, focus your attention on something else. Check in and see how you feel at the end of the week.

	WHAT COMPARISON DID YOU MAKE?	HOW DID YOU REFOCUS YOUR ATTENTION?
DAY 1		
DAY 2		
DAY 3		
DAY 4		
DAY 5		
DAY 6		
DAY 7		

It's the
imperfections
that make
things
beautiful.

—Jenny Han
AUTHOR

et's face it: Being mindful at home doesn't always work because you constantly see things that you have to do. At times like these, just switch off and let things go. Go out and explore a bit. What museums are on your wish list? What cities or neighborhoods would you like to visit on your own?

☐ Take a workshop or class.

☐ Watch a movie at an independent cinema or film center.

☐ Spend time browsing in a bookstore.

☐ Go to a lecture by a writer or an artist.

☐ Read at the library for a few hours.

☐ Get a pedicure.

☐ Sip tea at your favorite café.

☐

☐

☐

☐

☐

☐

☐

☐

☐

☐

☐

☐

☐

☐

spa
day

CHAPTER 3

My Perfectly Imperfect

FAMILY

A mindful family: Now, that sounds like a great idea. But in reality, it's easier said than done to keep all the plates spinning in our busy lives. Incorporating mindfulness into your family life can be as simple as making time for each other, whether your family life includes parents, children, or both. When a parent, partner, or child talks to you, look at that person, not your phone. But also don't try to keep everything under control. Embrace the chaos and try to maintain faith, a good sense of humor, and a sense of perspective. Your family won't do everything by the book—and neither will you. The most important ingredients for a mindful family life are patience, trust, and acceptance that things will always go differently from what you imagined.

Have a little more faith in things the way they are. Our minds can quickly turn facts into problems. In your head, a kid's birthday party has already failed because it's raining and you planned an outdoor treasure hunt. Trust that the children will have fun at the party and that they will enjoy themselves while watching a movie. Try to release control and focus more on how things are.

>> What's something in the past week that didn't go as planned? Was there a silver lining?

>> Make an herbarium with your children. (Search for beautiful petals and leaves that inspire you, dry them under a pile of books, stick them in a nice notebook, and jot down their names. Add a few short sentences about where you were and who you were with when you collected them.) Where in the neighborhood could you start collecting flowers and plants?

>> Have a picnic at a pleasant spot in the park with someone in your family and switch off your phones (or leave them at home for once). Did you pay more attention to each other when you didn't have your phones with you? Draw the picnic spot here. Or paste some blades of grass from your picnic spot, the label of a wine or lemonade bottle, or a piece of a napkin.

>> Organize a weekly movie night on the couch with your partner or child(ren)—or other housemates! Write down a list of films and TV series that you'd have fun watching together, and add ideas from your fellow viewer(s).

All that truly matters in the end is that you loved.

— Regina Brett
AUTHOR AND
NEWSPAPER COLUMNIST

Let go of the perfect image of your family. Every person is different, and sometimes life throws curveballs that no one saw coming. See things as they are: That's what mindfulness is all about. When you are worried or reacting to a story or an image, try to recognize what your mind is adding to the facts in front of you. Practice taking the story as it is.

» What makes your family perfectly imperfect?

» Breathe new life into the old-fashioned tradition of taking a drive. Where did you end up? Paste a memento here.

BOOK CLUB FOR TWO

Do you enjoy reading aloud to others? Even if you do not have children or they're already all grown up, reading to others or being read to—from a book or an article—can still be nice. You can't do it wrong: It's just a simple, relaxed moment, preferably with someone you like.

>> Which books would you like to read to someone? Or have read to you?

TITLE	AUTHOR

Things my partner/child loves

Things we both love

Things I love

>> Read your family a poem or a short text that moves you. Write the poem or the text here.

We all know we are capable of buying a birthday gift online while the TV is on *and* we are sending a text message *and* putting away dishes, but is it satisfying? Research has shown that we create half of our interruptions ourselves. Do you often feel the urge to get up and clean while you're working, or do you find yourself checking email while you're having breakfast? Take a deep breath and focus again on the one thing you were doing. This sharpens your mind and, over time, increases your capacity to concentrate longer on one thing.

>> Tiny pleasures I want to enjoy more:

Always . . . try to be a little kinder than is necessary.

—J. M. Barrie
AUTHOR AND PLAYWRIGHT

TRUE DIALOGUE

A nonjudgmental attitude is important in mindfulness. When you're listening carefully to your partner, try not to respond immediately with a reaction or judgment. When you embrace this attitude, the other person senses that you are fully present and that they have space to express what they're feeling, allowing a deeper conversation and connection to take place. True acceptance allows people the freedom to be who they are.

>> Take time out in the evening to drink a cup of tea or stroll around the neighborhood with your loved one. Write down your favorite parts of the conversation. How can you make a habit of carving out that time together?

CHAPTER 4

My Perfectly Imperfect
FRIENDS

We often take friendships for granted. Friends are always there when you need them, even if they haven't heard from you for weeks or months. But a good friendship also needs conscious attention. Mindfulness in friendships means that every now and then, you schedule in time and attention for a friend.

And while we want friendships to run smoothly, it's important to recognize that friends have their own lives and sometimes do things differently from how we would like or expect. Try not to pass judgment. Even saying *"Oh, me too!"* can halt the flow of that conversation. It's often better to let people tell their story in peace and ask them questions about anything that's unclear. When you are listening, you don't have to say much.

>> Everyone has off days now and then, so remember to be patient with yourself during those times. What would you say to a friend in the same situation? What would you say to yourself? Do you notice a difference?

WHAT WOULD I SAY TO A FRIEND?	WHAT WOULD I SAY TO MYSELF?

off day

EMPATHY IN FRIENDSHIP

Next time you're in a conversation with someone who's going through a hard time, try to really understand, without judging, what the other person is feeling: How would you feel if you were in his or her place? What emotions might this person be experiencing? If you are able to get a sense of that, you'll be making real contact and it will be easier for you to know what might help—based not on your perspective or preconceptions, but on the other person's feelings. When you're able to find the best way to help, the consolation feels sincere and strengthens your bond.

>> Recall the last time you made real contact with a friend. Were you able to listen—really listen?

When hosting friends or family, let the event unfold naturally. (This works in life, too.) Of course you can put your best foot forward, but if you try to be the hostess with the mostest, you'll probably just end up stressing yourself out—no fun for you and no fun for your guests either. So just take things as they come and try to see the humor in any "failures."

>> Write about an event or experience that didn't go as planned and now makes you laugh when you reminisce about it.

Happiness depends on the quality of the attention you give to yourself, to others, and to the world.

—Frédéric Lenoir
PHILOSOPHER

HOW YOU PLAY THE GAME

Do you always want to win? Sometimes you might forget that you can have fun simply by playing a game—because you like to be with others and spend time off your screen. Of course you would rather win, but how bad is it to lose now and then?

>> Write down the games you would like to play just for the fun of it and with whom.

ook upon your friends with mildness and leniency and respond to them with empathy and understanding. Do not be too strict. Is your love suddenly gone if your friend makes a mistake, doesn't follow through on an agreement, or is in a bad mood? Or do you still love them just as much as before? Try to deal with yourself in the same way: friendly, attentive, and forgiving.

>> Think of someone special and write a list of all the qualities you love about that person. Then do the same for yourself.

NAME: _____   ME

>> Listen to your favorite music and enjoy a special drink while doing so. Draw whatever your mind wanders to.

>> Set an annual tradition with friends, such as taking a long bike ride. Choose a route in advance and draw it here.

A SHIFT IN PERSPECTIVE

As humans we are naturally inclined to see where we stand on the social ladder. We also tend to obsess about the people who are doing just a little better than we are because we think we can catch up with them if we just do *more*. But there is no end to the number of people who are more beautiful, more intelligent, or more creative than we are. Even if we catch up with them, there will always be people doing better. In short, it doesn't do us any good to think like that.

>> Plan a creative weekend with a friend (attend a sculpture workshop, for example). That way you'll be doing something together but will also have time and space for your own project. Write down your favorite parts of the weekend.

We do not need magic to transform our world; we carry all the power we need inside ourselves already.

— J. K. Rowling
AUTHOR

Our schedules often fill up so quickly with appointments, family commitments, and work that it can be hard to find time to simply hang out with friends. But when we do make the effort, that quality time filled with laughter and good conversation leaves us feeling loved and refreshed. Carving out these moments is not only good for our relationships, but our minds.

» If you can, take a day off work during the week and visit someplace new with a friend. Write here a list of places you both would enjoy.

>> Write down the names of classes you would like to take and with whom. Find out when they are being offered, and write an invitation to your friend to join you.

CLASS	WITH	WHEN	NOTES

>> Go to a flea market with a friend early one morning. Reflect on your experience afterward. What difference did going early make? If it wasn't as busy as usual, did you pay more attention to each other?

Maybe it bothers you that other people don't notice when you're asking for help. But have you been clear enough? Could you ask for help more directly? Or turn it around: Doing something kind for someone else can often make you feel better.

WHAT CAN YOU ASK FOR?	WHAT CAN YOU OFFER?

CHAPTER 5

My Perfectly Imperfect

ADVENTURES

You've worked so hard for months that you haven't had any time for yourself, and now you're finally on vacation. But once you arrive at the beach, it turns out to be crowded every day and the nearest supermarket is ten miles away. Restful? Not really. Just as in your everyday life, you will have days that are successful and days that don't work out.

It's no coincidence that the word *vacation* comes from the Latin word *vaco*, which means "vacant" or "unoccupied." Imagine how lovely it would be to decide what you want to do (or not) when you wake up, to shape your day based on how you feel at that moment instead of on a premeditated idea. Starting new adventures with an open mind (and no to-do list) and looking at things through the eyes of a novice can really help. The obstacles and side steps along the way turn into tiny little adventures, which you can always expand upon.

It doesn't always have to be something big and overwhelming. (And it needn't involve traveling, necessarily!) Something as small as choosing a different ice cream flavor can make you feel adventurous.

GO ON A TRIP

According to René Descartes, the philosopher of doubt, going on vacation—no matter how short—is a good way to examine your life. On vacation, you are distanced from your home base, your securities. Descartes believed that this was the best way to acquire wisdom. Outside your safety zone, you get to know yourself better. You make new contacts, you deviate from your daily routine, perhaps even become acquainted with a different culture. All those experiences can help you examine your true feelings about yourself and your life at home.

What do I really like?

What makes me happy?

What do I want to change?

W hat do you usually have for lunch? When you're traveling, trying something new is part of the adventure. It can be something small, like a different kind of sandwich, a new type of tea, or a spice that you haven't used before.

>> What did you try today that was new?

>> When you go on a day trip or out of town for a few days, tell your family and friends that you can be reached only in an emergency. Reflect on it afterward. How did it feel?

TIME IS ELASTIC

In Indonesia, people understand the slow life. They even have a special term for it: *jam karet*, which literally means "elastic time." According to the Indonesians, time can stretch in all directions. In practice, this means that an appointment for 3:00 p.m. sharp never begins on time. It can just as easily start fifteen minutes later, or at 4:00 p.m. No one gets stressed by the constraints of time, and no one is offended if you turn up late.

>> Try setting the dining table with some beautiful tableware on the weekend. It'll feel like you're on vacation when time feels like a luxury, yet you'll get to sleep in your own bed. Draw how your table looked (before and after dinner).

Before

After

One of the basic principles of mindfulness is approaching life with an open outlook. A vacation, a visit to another city, or just shopping in a different supermarket is a perfect opportunity to practice that fresh perspective. If you're visiting a place that is new, allow yourself to discover and absorb everything. Let go of judgments, just be in the moment, and let all of your senses do the work.

>> How does it smell here?

>> What sounds do you hear?

>> What new colors and patterns do you see?

>> Close your eyes and describe what you *feel*.

5 Tips for Breaking Out of Your Routine

1 Speak the truth (without being hurtful).

2 Try a new sport or activity.

3 Write a letter to someone you admire.

4 Take a day off for no reason.

5 Keep a journal (see chart, opposite).

>> American psychologist Roy Baumeister suggests keeping a journal. Pick out behaviors you would like to change and then determine those that would be easiest to adjust. Write down your goals and record what you are doing in detail.

BEHAVIOR TO CHANGE	GOALS	ACTIONS

Happiness is not a station you arrive at, but a manner of traveling.

—Margaret Lee Runbeck

AUTHOR

Go for a walk. Focus your attention on your feet, from the moment your heel hits the ground until your foot rolls forward and moves through the air again. Pay attention to how the other foot is automatically set in motion.

» Draw your route here.

>> What went wrong today? And . . . did you manage to laugh at yourself rather than get angry with yourself?

>> What drink do you order most frequently in a café? Try something different. You may discover a new favorite. Draw your drink here.

LITTLE STEPS, BIG STEPS

Some changes come in small steps; others come in grander gestures. Whether big or small, the change is what's important—it will help you gain a new perspective wherever your feet are planted.

>> What small daily things could you do differently? (For example, you might take a new route to work or have lunch with a different colleague.)

>> Is there also something bigger, or more significant, that you would like to do differently?

>> Which days this week will you do them?

>> How and when could that happen?

LOOK TO THE PAST, LOOK TO THE FUTURE

Another way to gain perspective in the present is to reflect on previous experiences and set goals for the future.

» Looking back on the last five years, is there anything that you wish you had done differently?

» Might you be more successful at doing them differently now?

» What new things would you still like to learn?

» Are there things you tried to change previously that didn't work out?

» What are you going to do differently as of tomorrow?

» Going for a walk in the park without taking your phone almost constitutes a proper adventure nowadays. Whoever wants to reach you will just have to try again later. You are off the radar. If you see a beautiful flower, you can pick it (instead of photographing and sharing it on Instagram). Dry it in the pages of a book and then glue it onto this page, with a little drawing of the place you found it.

Anything that is new—
it can be a museum
exhibition or a workshop in
watercolor painting, flower
arranging, whatever—helps
to get you thinking out
of the box, while you are
also being fed new ideas,
knowledge, and images.

—Danny Penman

AUTHOR AND MINDFULNESS EXPERT

When you're on vacation or doing something else for pleasure, try embracing a "nonstriving" attitude. See what comes your way, rather than trying to see and do everything. You might find that you enjoy yourself even more because of the unexpected things that pop up. But for that to happen, you have to give chance a chance.

>> As you embark on a new adventure, what is the first thing to come to mind that excites you? Follow that whim! Later, reflect on your experience. Did you discover something you otherwise would've missed?

Doing something new—like learning a new language, traveling to a new place, or eating in a restaurant you've never been to before—can make you feel like time is slowing down. What's more, memories slow down time, so try to savor these adventures. Start at dinner tonight and taste your meal as if you've never tasted anything like it before.

>> What's the texture like?

>> What flavors does it have?

>> Describe the aroma.

>> What colors do you see on your plate?

BREAK OUT OF YOUR COMFORT ZONE

Everybody's comfort zone is a little different. Ask around: One person may be able to effortlessly speak to a roomful of people but won't want to leave the country when vacation time comes around; someone else may feel intimidated by the idea of talking with a stranger but have no problem traveling all over the globe. And then there's the matter of how *far* you want to stray from your comfort zone. You don't have to break free entirely; you can stretch daily routines out a little at a time. For example, try talking to a stranger, going to the movies on your own, cooking with new ingredients once a week, or picking a book merely by intuition instead of choosing something off the bestseller list.

>> Reflect on your experience afterward. How did it go?

CHAPTER 6

My Perfectly Imperfect

CREATIVITY

From drawing to baking an apple pie, being creative is a way to clear your mind. Tinkering with something slows down the constant flow of thoughts, and if you approach activities in a mindful way, they become less about the result and more about the process. And isn't it much nicer to have a singularly imperfect homemade pillow than a perfectly manufactured item that has rolled off a production line? *Handcrafted* and *authentic* are the magic words here; let them be the special characteristics that bring together the average DIY project. Celebrate imperfection, enjoy the process, and surprise yourself.

Unless you are making things for a living, it's not about the result. Why shouldn't we still be able to fold, cut, draw, and color, just like we did when we were children, without it having to be something in particular? Let go of your expectations and be okay with the fact that your project may end up in the back of a closet. You are still honing your creativity even if the result isn't 100 percent perfect.

PROJECT IMPERFECTION

Making something with your hands, whether knitting, crocheting, gardening, or papering a wall, is a valuable exercise in letting perfectionism go. Did you know that handmade Persian rugs and Japanese kimonos are intentionally created with at least one "flaw" by their makers? According to custom, the only entity who doesn't make mistakes is God (or whatever name you give your deity). Going easy on yourself is useful in completing any DIY project: Be reasonable in your expectations, honor the learning curve if there is one, and embrace the process over the result.

PROJECTS YOU HAVEN'T FINISHED BECAUSE YOU APPROACHED THEM WITH TOO MUCH PERFECTIONISM	HOW CAN YOU LOOK AT THEM AGAIN, THIS TIME WITH A MILDER EYE?
1 _____ _____	⟩ _____ _____
2 _____ _____	⟩ _____ _____
3 _____ _____	⟩ _____ _____
4 _____ _____	⟩ _____ _____

ALWAYS LEARNING

DIY becomes a lot more fun and relaxed when you focus on learning the craft and not on how much time you're spending on it. Challenge yourself with realistic goals, and do not set the bar too high. Something like knitting socks requires an advanced technique that you won't learn in an instant. It takes a great deal of dedication and many hours, if not years, before you master it. But how can you keep the process gratifying if you can do only a little? Well, using meaningful materials, for example, can raise the level of enjoyment. Maybe your friend gave you some special yarn for your birthday, or maybe you're making a quilt out of old T-shirts. Using materials with sentimental value can change your whole experience.

WHAT ARE SOME REALISTIC GOALS YOU CAN SET FOR YOURSELF?	WHAT MATERIALS WILL YOU USE?

>> What is the most messed-up dessert you've ever baked? Draw it here. How did it taste?

CREATIVE CHALLENGE

When you're heading home from work, it's normal to be pretty wrapped up in various worries—about the day, about what you still have to do tomorrow, about dinner. Put those worries aside on your commute, and replace them with a search for something beautiful. If you're walking, stop to notice exceptional front doors (and snap pictures of them!). If you're taking the bus or train, enjoy the relative quiet to finally finish that chapter you've been reading. If you're driving, notice new buildings or spot some greenery at the next stop light. When you're searching for something specific, you have less time to focus on unpleasantness—and you may just discover a whole new view of your city, a favorite book, or an inspiring article.

>> Chart your commute experience for five days. How did it evolve throughout the week? How did you spend your commute? What did you discover?

	HOW DID YOU SPEND YOUR COMMUTE?	WHAT DID YOU DISCOVER?
DAY 1		
DAY 2		
DAY 3		
DAY 4		
DAY 5		

no need to hurry

We are born to dream and make the things we dream about.

—Nicola Yoon
AUTHOR

What comes naturally to creative people—seeing and feeling with all their senses—can be learned through mindfulness. If you focus on everyday occurrences with your full attention, you'll notice interesting images and exciting ideas that you otherwise would've missed, and you'll begin to see them more quickly.

>> What did you notice today, after seeing and feeling with all your senses?

PEACE OF MIND

Drawing a sketch, sewing a pillowcase, crocheting a granny square, knitting a scarf. . . . If your mind is always crammed full of thoughts, you'll appreciate being mindlessly busy when you do something with your hands—just "being." Scientific studies show that you often make better decisions if you focus on something other than your thoughts for a bit and let your subconscious do the work.

>> Write down the ideas you had this week as you worked with your hands instead of your head.

"The negative thoughts that were streaming through my head are deadly for creativity," says Danny Penman, a British mindfulness expert and author of the book *Mindfulness for Creativity*. "When you have a snide comment for everything you're doing, you're not giving creative thoughts a chance," he says. "You won't notice them or you will instantly dismiss them as silly ideas: not good enough."

When a foolish and counterproductive thought passes by (*You're stupid; they'll probably think your ideas are silly*), you can choose to ignore it in a friendly manner. By letting go, your mind becomes lighter and more relaxed. You are no longer trapped by thoughts that strangle every creative impulse. By stepping out of this obstructive spiral of thoughts, you regain control over your direction.

>> How did this work for you today?

MINDFUL WRITING

Writing can be a form of meditation. Start with the sentence "Right now, I am aware of . . ." and write down everything that occurs to you. For example, "I know that I am sitting on a chair, I have a headache, and I want a cup of coffee." Don't write down things from the past or the future, just what is going on at this very moment. If you run out of things to write about, write *that* down.

» Right now, I am aware of:

_____

_____

_____

_____

_____

_____

_____

_____

_____

_____

_____

_____

_____

_____

_____

_____

you are perfectly imperfect.

We all learn great techniques in kindergarten: papier-mâché, collage, working with pastels, painting with watercolors, and much more. Although many of us once loved these crafts, somehow on our way to adulthood we lost our lack of inhibition and became much more critical of our mistakes. Too often people say, "I'm actually not very creative" or "I'm no good at this." But once you've spent about half an hour working with paper, for example, you really get into a flow; that's the best way to describe it. That's what paper can do. What was your favorite craft when you were a kid?

>> Give yourself thirty minutes to play around with craft materials today, and brainstorm some ideas here about things you can make.

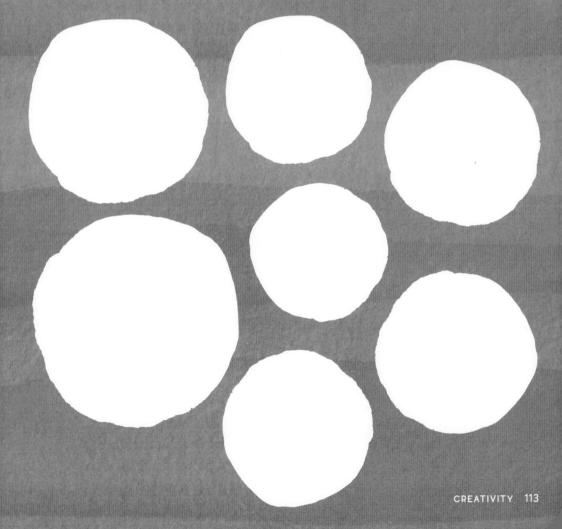

CHARMING MISTAKES

"I love paper so much that I always feel a little lost if I don't have any within reach," says French illustrator and paper artist Julie Marabelle, who lives in Amsterdam. "If you make a crooked cut by accident, you can't fix it, and it's noticeable," she says. "But a mistake has a certain charm, and that's why it always works out. Sometimes, the end result is even better for it."

>> Do you have a favorite object that has a flaw or two? What do you like most about that object?

A creative date is not a selfish act; it's a necessity. Your mind as well as your body needs to be nourished. Mindfulness expert Danny Penman actually says a solo date should be a permanent fixture on everyone's to-do list. Write down the things you would like to do on a creative solo date (the activity can be anything: visiting an art gallery, going mountain climbing, or walking through a new city—or a new neighborhood in your city).

1. _____

2. _____

3. _____

4. _____

5. _____

6. _____

7. _____

8. _____

9. _____

10. _____

D o you ever go on vacation and realize that there are just so many beautiful things to see that there's no way you could possibly see them all? Taking photographs of just one subject can be a mindful way to approach this situation. By picking one category to focus on, you feel more centered.

>> What subject do you like to photograph? What's your most interesting shot?

ALONE TIME

It's a classic tale: Scientists and artists reach their most brilliant insights in the moments when they aren't focusing at all. As Mozart wrote in one of his letters: "When I am, as it were, completely myself, entirely alone, and of good cheer—say traveling in a carriage, or walking after a good meal, or during the night when I cannot sleep; it is on such occasions that my ideas flow best and most abundantly."

>> Forcing yourself to focus on something often has the opposite effect. Creativity needs time, rest, and space. Write down what you've been stuck on lately and something you can do to take your mind off it.

WHAT YOU'VE BEEN STUCK ON	WHAT YOU CAN DO TO TAKE YOUR MIND OFF IT

I don't know so well what I think until I see what I say.

—Flannery O'Connor

AUTHOR

There are similarities between working with paper and mindfulness. Tearing paper, for example, is hard to do carefully, so you allow yourself space and freedom during the process. Suddenly you see what you've made and realize it actually turned out pretty great—this often leads to new, creative ideas. If you regularly do creative work and learn how to appreciate the "mistakes," you will cultivate a more open outlook on life.

"Paper is very accessible, and I personally get most of my inspiration from everyday objects," Dutch designer Lisa Manuels says. "The Dutch city of Rotterdam sends its mail in these gorgeous mint-green envelopes—really nice paper. Sometimes you can even take something ugly, like a free leaflet, and turn it into something beautiful."

>> What everyday objects can you collect and use?

CREATIVE CHALLENGE

Themed photographs are a fun way to get creative within your day-to-day life. Try photographing a different detail of your house every day for thirty days and posting the photos on social media to keep track of your progress. This project will give you a healthy new perspective on your home (*Oh, that doorknob is actually quite beautiful. I never noticed it before*).

» Write down a list of everything you photographed over the thirty days and any special details that you hadn't noticed before.

1	2	3
4	5	6
7	8	9
10	11	12

13

14

15

16

17

18

19

20

21

22

23

24

25

26

27

28

29

30

CHAPTER 7

My Perfectly Imperfect BODY

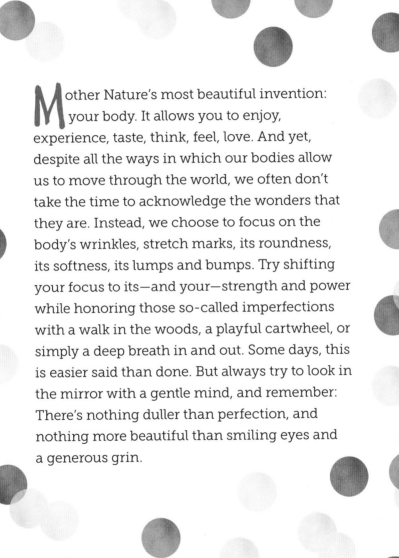

Mother Nature's most beautiful invention: your body. It allows you to enjoy, experience, taste, think, feel, love. And yet, despite all the ways in which our bodies allow us to move through the world, we often don't take the time to acknowledge the wonders that they are. Instead, we choose to focus on the body's wrinkles, stretch marks, its roundness, its softness, its lumps and bumps. Try shifting your focus to its—and your—strength and power while honoring those so-called imperfections with a walk in the woods, a playful cartwheel, or simply a deep breath in and out. Some days, this is easier said than done. But always try to look in the mirror with a gentle mind, and remember: There's nothing duller than perfection, and nothing more beautiful than smiling eyes and a generous grin.

RUNNING MEDITATION

Running is an ideal way to "leave your head." To not think of work, your child's school project, or what is on your agenda, but to focus on the now: *I am running here. I am experiencing this.* Try it without music, which often serves only as a distraction. Instead, try to feel your body while running. Experience what is happening.

>> How was your breathing? What feeling did you have in your feet?

Walking in nature is good for the body and soul. Along with his research team, Professor Yoshifumi Miyazaki of the Center for Environment, Health, and Field Sciences at Chiba University in Japan conducted an extensive study on the effect of walking in forests compared with walking through busy city centers. You guessed it: The woodland hikers felt more relaxed than the city walkers. Their levels of the stress hormone cortisol also decreased significantly, as well as their blood pressure and heart rate. That's why Miyazaki advises everyone to take a regular "forest bath."

≫ Stick a leaf here that you found during a walk. Write a sentence about how you felt when you found it.

Being active every day makes it easier to hear that inner voice.

—Haruki Murakami

AUTHOR

A BIT OF FRESH AIR

Shinrin-yoku, translated as "taking in the forest atmosphere," was developed in Japan in 1982 to promote the health of city dwellers. According to Japanese scientists, it is not only the fresh air that is beneficial, but also the natural essential oils, called phytoncides, that are emitted by the trees and plants. *Shinrin-yoku* has all kinds of positive influences on our health: It improves mood, reduces stress, and reduces the risk of cardiovascular disease.

The great thing about going for a walk is that you can use all your senses: Feel the wind, touch the trees, sniff the smells, register all the colors around you. . . . Those are things that we sometimes forget to notice.

>> Plan a walk (it doesn't have to be long). Write down how you experienced it.

A Simple Breathing Exercise

Step 1

Sit down. Close your eyes. Observe your thoughts, your body, your mood.

Step 2

Feel your entire body and then begin to notice your breathing. Don't do anything to change it.

Step 3

Allow your breath to go through your whole body and then turn your attention to the space around you. What do you hear, what do you smell, what do you feel? Open your eyes again.

» Write down whatever comes to your mind here.

_____

_____

_____

_____

_____

Sometimes it seems like running is almost a competition with yourself. You have to go a certain distance in a certain amount of time, you have to go as often as possible, you need to run a marathon at least once, and you have to train hard for it. But when running is not a contest, you run for your own pleasure. Then, running becomes about the movement and what you encounter along the way. If you see a beautiful rainbow, it's best to stop and look at it for a while—and running slowly is okay, too.

>> Did you manage to stop during your run (or other form of exercise)? What did you see?

JUST ENJOY IT

Ignore others and do what makes you feel good when it comes to exercise. Begin with something that you find manageable, just to get yourself moving. And don't do it to win or to share on social media— just enjoy it. If you set more and more goals, then you may lose sight of the joy that comes with simply doing it.

» If you don't enjoy doing something, you'll never find the motivation to continue doing it. What's a physical activity that you enjoy and can commit to once a week?

What I know for sure is that pleasure is energy reciprocated: What you put out comes back.

—Oprah Winfrey
MEDIA MOGUL

Swimming brings you into the here and now and can take away tension in your mind and body. It is the ideal sport to become aware of your breathing. Maybe you know someone who's done a polar bear plunge—an event where participants swim in the winter, when water is at its coldest. Or maybe you've done one yourself! If you have, you know that the swim makes you feel more alive than ever before. When you step out of the water and your blood is pumping through your body, you feel *strong*.

» When's the last time you felt strong? What made you feel that way?

A LITTLE R&R

There's nothing wrong with working hard, but not allowing your body to get the rest it needs is not okay. It's important to have the right balance between expending your energy and replenishing it. Make sure you stop what you are doing on a regular and timely basis, take a step back, and, most of all, schedule time for rest.

» Be loyal to your body: Listen to it carefully and take it seriously. Feel through your senses: Let the wind blow through your hair, feel the sun on your skin, or walk barefoot on the sand. And be aware of what your senses are telling you. What do you smell, what do you taste? Make sure you stay in touch with your body.

WHAT DO YOU TASTE?	WHAT DO YOU TOUCH?
WHAT DO YOU SEE?	
WHAT DO YOU SMELL?	WHAT DO YOU HEAR?

WHAT CAN YOU DO IF YOU'RE FEELING TOO STRESSED?

- Accept that stress belongs to life. If you feel tired, irritable, or exhausted, give yourself space and air.

- Do only what is absolutely necessary. Remove everything that does not necessarily have to get done from your to-do list, in both your work and your personal life. Make sure to accept social invitations only once you've evaluated your emotions. Sometimes events and activities may sound relaxing but can actually cost more energy than you think.

- Make sure you sleep well. Slowing down in the evening helps you fall asleep: Listen to gentle music, read a book, drink herbal tea. And get into the habit of doing some relaxing breathing exercises before you go to bed.

- Do not view stress as an enemy, but as a fascinating process that you can learn from by listening to your body and mind.

Are you able to walk or bike somewhere instead of driving? Looking at the landscape through a car window—like a kind of film that is passing you by—is pleasant, but sometimes it is even more pleasant to be part of it.

》 Describe a recent time that you were part of the landscape and not just a spectator.

Swiss-born French philosopher Jean-Jacques Rousseau claimed that he could think properly only when he walked alone. In nature, his inspiration flowed freely, whereas the sight of his writing desk made him feel overcome by aversion and boredom.

Whenever you have a chance to go outside, grab it. For example, if you know that the weather will be good in the next few days, try to organize your work so that you will have a weekday morning free to go for a walk (maybe even walk to work!).

>> When can you fit a walk into your weekly schedule?

I will not follow
where the path
may lead
but I will go
where there is no path
and I will leave a trail.

— Muriel Strode
POET

HOW TO GET MOVING

- Find an activity you enjoy doing. Maybe you're more of dancer than a runner, or you have a passion for tennis. Figuring out what you love is the first step.

- Don't start out too fanatically. Before you know it, you may get injured or feel defeated and stop because your expectations are too high.

- Invite a friend or two. Doing activities together will help you stay motivated, and you'll have a lot more fun.

- Make exercise part of your daily life: Skipping the elevator and taking the stairs, carrying shopping bags, biking against the wind, and cleaning your windows all count as exercise.

- Making time for thirty minutes of physical activity when you still have a huge to-do list is not a waste of time. Our working memory has a limited capacity. After an active break, you'll be twice as efficient.

CHAPTER 8

My Perfectly Imperfect SELF

Even when things seem to be going well, it can be hard for many to see the glass as half full. Worrying about what others think of you, thinking about how things will go wrong, and doubting anything and everything are not uncommon thoughts.

Sometimes it seems like huge, idealistic changes are necessary to flip your life around and allow you to be happy. But small changes often have a big effect. The next time you start feeling overwhelmed by negative thoughts, remember this: You are imperfect. You make mistakes. You may even make the same mistakes over and over (and over!) again. *And that's okay.*

WHAT WAS NOT PERFECT TODAY?	HOW DID THAT FEEL?

BE KIND (TO YOURSELF)

Slowing down also means being kind to yourself. You're allowed to just relax on the couch with a cup of tea.

>> Draw yourself in your favorite place to simply be.

>> Write a letter to your not-so-perfect self.

Dear _____ ,

With affection,

>> Today, for a change, don't make a list of all the practical and urgent things you need to do. Instead, make a list here of the things you'd still like to do this week: Give the cat a big cuddle, take an evening stroll, frame drawings (your children's or your own) . . . anything that brings you joy.

my best listener

HEADS OR TAILS

If you're in doubt about something small, it may not actually matter what decision you make. A lot of doubts stem from a lack of differences. If a sensible alternative were available, you would know what decision to make. If necessary, choose with your eyes closed or flip a coin. And if you secretly wish that the coin had landed on heads instead of tails (or vice versa), you'll know what you truly want.

>> Make a list of some upcoming small decisions. Can you apply an element of chance to them to relieve some pressure?

» What did you do today in haste that you could have done more slowly?

>> What character trait would you like to have? Are you sure you don't already possess a little of this trait?

>> And ultimately, how bad is it that you don't have that characteristic? What are some other character traits that make you *you*?

>> Do not let the fear of getting something wrong, which will inevitably happen when you try something new, stop you from learning new things. What was the last thing you did for the first time?

>> Make a list of your guilty pleasures here. Can you make time to indulge in one this week?

Just try to be happy. Unhappiness starts with wanting to be happier.

—Sam Levenson
HUMORIST AND WRITER

>> Jot down a few everyday things that make you happy for no reason at all.

Although the internet has made our world smaller, it's also made more things available for comparison. So, you come across the best outfits and perfectly styled homes on your social media feeds. And you start thinking, *Hmm . . . mine's not as good, so why even bother?* Try not to get distracted by what other people do or think—just use your feeds for inspiration. Above all, listen to your own feelings and do what makes you happy.

>> Cut out a picture from a magazine (or make a drawing) of something that you like—a garden full of flowers, an unusual bathroom, a cupboard full of beautiful crockery—and paste it here. Don't view it as something you do not have and someone else does, but use it as inspiration.

>> To whom were you extra kind today?

>> In what ways were you extra kind to yourself?

GOOD VS. BEST

Sometimes you have to bite the bullet and make a choice. This can be hard for the so-called maximizers among us, who are always looking for the best product, the highest achievable goal, and the fanciest alternative. A typical maximizer can easily spend a week deliberating over a new bike or a juicer. Booking a vacation can be a major drama. With every option comes a new objection. The question maximizers ask themselves—*Is this the best option?*—is an impossible one because they will never know the answer. A better question to ask is *"Is this a good option?"* That way, the bar is lowered, which eases decision-making.

>> What dilemmas are you currently facing? Which ones can you address by choosing a "good option"?

>> It can be absolutely blissful to stretch out on the couch and watch your favorite show. Try it, and if you're unable to shake that guilty feeling, take a walk afterward to get some fresh air. But in the meantime, what are your favorite television shows, series, or films?

>> When was the last time you petted an animal?

Here was peace. She pulled in her horizon like a great fish-net. Pulled it from around the waist of the world and draped it over her shoulder. So much of life in its meshes! She called in her soul to come and see.

—Zora Neale Hurston

AUTHOR AND ANTHROPOLOGIST

>> What would you say to a child who is trying things out and developing a sense of the world?

>> What would you say to yourself if you tried something new and it didn't work?

>> Are you addicted to your phone? If so, remember this adage: Out of sight, out of mind. Get into the habit of regularly keeping your phone in your coat pocket or in your bag, and switch it to silent mode. Leave your phone on this page and go do something fun.

Sometimes your head is just too full, with all kinds of thoughts creeping around in it. One way to help clear your head is to tidy something up or do a clean-out. For example, empty a kitchen cupboard, clean it, and organize all the spice jars in it. Or open up a kitchen drawer, clear it out, and then put all the utensils back in an orderly fashion. Sometimes it really works: A tidy cupboard = a tidy mind.

>> Make a list of all the tiny areas you could reorganize. Next time you're in need of a mental cleanse, tackle one of these.

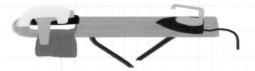

Things that make me happy

» Things that give me energy

>> Habits I want to break

Things I want to let go of

» Are you angry, tired, or stressed? What are your favorite ways to cheer yourself up?

ABOUT THE AUTHORS

Irene Smit and *Astrid van der Hulst* are the creative directors of *Flow* magazine, a popular international publication packed with paper goodies and beautiful illustrations celebrating creativity, imperfection, and life's little pleasures. Irene and Astrid began their magazine careers as editors at *Cosmopolitan* and *Marie Claire*. In 2008, inspired by their passion for paper and quest for mindfulness, they dreamed up the idea for their own magazine in a small attic. They are now the coauthors of seven books, including *A Book That Takes Its Time*, *The Tiny Book of Tiny Pleasures*, *Creativity Takes Courage*, and *The Big Book of Less*. They each live with their families in Haarlem, the Netherlands. To see more of their work, visit flowmagazine.com.

ABOUT THE ILLUSTRATOR

Karen Weening has been working as an illustrator for five years, but she has been drawing all her life. With a background in urban planning, she is often inspired by architecture and the use of land and city spaces, and can often be found outside on her bicycle. Her subjects range from beautiful interiors to winter sweaters and greenhouses full of plants. The theme of this book suits Karen, she says, because "it's about daily life and its beauty. Sometimes I need to be reminded of that. I learn a lot from my children, for whom the glass always seems half full. I hope they can hold on to that perspective throughout their lives." She lives with her family outside Amsterdam.